MY DEAD

AMY LAWLESS'
MY DEAD

OCTOPUS BOOKS 2013
PORTLAND   DENVER   OMAHA

M Y   D E A D

BY AMY LAWLESS

© COPYRIGHT **2013**

ALL RIGHTS RESERVED

PUBLISHED BY OCTOPUS BOOKS

OCTOPUSBOOKS.NET

PORTLAND, DENVER, OMAHA

ISBN **978-0-9851182-3-5**

FIRST EDITION

OCTOPUS BOOKS IS DISTRIBUTED BY

SMALL PRESS DISTRIBUTION

SPDBOOKS.ORG

PRINTED BY THOMSON-SHORE INC.

IN THE UNITED STATES

COVER DESIGN BY RICK DELUCCO

DESIGNED AND SET BY DREW SCOTT SWENHAUGEN

TEXT SET IN BARIOL AND SCOTCH ROMAN

FOR THOSE WHO ARE NO LONGER HERE

ELEPHANTS IN MOURNING

FOR MARTIN LEONARD

Elephants come across an elephant carcass in the wild.
They gather in a defensive circle around the bones and rotted
Flesh. They pick up a bone and another bone. They rub the bones
With their trunks. They touch each bone with a hind foot.
They investigate each part of the body,
Put the bone in the mouth like a cigarette and
Looks like it's smoking it.
For a moment I feel like I'm watching detectives gnawing
On a new case.

This means something.
One day my matter will return to the land.
The water in my body disperses
And isn't replaced with new tap water.
Let's all drink to the death of a clown.
The water will go into leaves.
What can I leave here?
There was a ritual, and now she is gone.
Visit remains.

When an elephant dies

The lover will approach and stand there.

When an elephant dies he tries to necessitate the other elephant.

This is called searching for meaning.

When a human dies

A person who's spent a hundred thousand dollars on medical school

Will confirm that

Something is gone.

Spirit? Animus? Evelyn?

Something left the room.

And now here is matter. Calories of energy.

Rotted DNA. Hair thinned.

Once the oxygen hits it will be red.

Once my grandmother told me that if a needle got into my bloodstream

It would pierce my heart and I'd die.

This made no sense but her passion convinced me.

I feared needles.

Why couldn't I have been encouraged to be bold?

Why was I encouraged to be afraid?

When an elephant dies the lover takes the body and rolls it over and over.

When an elephant is dead it lies in a way that living elephants can not.

When an elephant dies he takes the body and rolls it over.

He scrolls his trunk and pulls his head back.

Some call that honor but it looks like someone who wants religion for a minute.

He does not x out the window.

He is someone who wants to be told that there is something else.

There is nothing else.

When an elephant dies he's in your house during one of his episodes. He's gotten you pregnant so you're his and he goes wild. When an elephant dies it's important to know the types of leaves there are in the world. The water in this elephant will leave it and go into the leaves and also into our faucets. The water will go into our water filtration systems. The water will go into our clouds and will rain on our faces. The water will go into your sex lubricant bottles. The water will go into the sewers of Dubai and the mountains of Africa. The waters will go into the snowcapped Rockies of Colorado. The waters will go to every hill and molehill of Mississippi. When an elephant dies it's important to list the different kinds of leaves, which you can find in plant matter and botany textbooks: fronds, conifers, angiosperms, microphylls, sheaths, and specialized.

When an elephant dies you want to be immediately pregnant so you can feel the huge cessation of Earth life while stroking your own belly and its hugeness. When an elephant dies they are all emotionally affected and you are emotionally affected unless you have a condition or you were born that way or you have Alzheimer's. Elephants are known for their memories. But you've been surfing the internet and not paying attention. You've been watching TV, eating candy, and texting jokes with your best friend. You're also cooking a batch of cookies. Pay attention. Pay attention. I'm only going to say this once.

When an elephant dies you immediately want to hug everyone around you. But first put the bone in your mouth and feel around for clues. Was it a violent death? Was it natural? Yell something hurtful to your brother because he isn't even putting his hind leg against the edge of the dried skin area of the head. He's still smelling it with his trunk. If you say something slightly hurtful to your brother he'll stop slacking off with the smell segment, which is an overrated line of analysis. We find the most important diagnostic cues by hind foot tapping and tasting. My wife made a trumpet noise so at least she clearly gives a shit. This is my daughter's first dead body. This is how it's done, sweetie. We're going to find out who did this to this poor woman. Time did this. Watch me kill time.

When an elephant dies
Please don't eat chips in the corner after a five hour-long wake
Because the daughter will take her trunk
And beat you with verbs and nouns.

When an elephant dies
Sometimes the remaining elephants become distressed
Because there's no evidence of an afterlife.

People like the word faith.
Elephants don't.

When an elephant dies
Sometimes all you have to do is be there
And no one will judge you
If you don't say something witty.

Sometimes when an elephant dies
I want to grab a bunch of scientists
And one scientist will wipe the tear
Out of the elephant's eye
And say "I can explain" and draw the bone
From the mouth of the living.
Scientists are people who can explain things
To us. They have brain matter and
Access to tools that elephants don't have.
I can explain, one will say.

But getting an elephant to let go of the bone
Is an entirely different matter.

Sometimes a slew of elephants die,

And you're dealing with what is called a massacre.

When three thousand die maybe you have to just

Watch a movie.

It reminds me of biology class in eleventh grade.

The combination of math

And chemistry were too much and, boy, I gave up.

Mourning a grandmother is one thing.

Mourning three thousand someone's child is too much,

But we do it anyway by

Watching some DVD until it's over

And then letting it sit on the coffee table for a week

Until you can get out of bed and look at it

Not recognizing that this cultural artifact will always be the thing I did

Instead of watch news that day in September.

Sometimes an elephant dies and no one finds him and his flesh dries off his bones and the bones slowly absorb back into the land and later a farmer will till the land and grow crops and the crops will feed the family and the family will grow up and old and no one will know that they used to be elephants.

Sometimes a man dies and no one finds him and his flesh dries off his bones and the bones slowly absorb back into the land and later a farmer will till the land and grow crops and the crops will feed the family and the family will grow up and old and no one will know that they used to be man.

Sometimes a man dies and someone finds him and his flesh has dried off his bones and the bones slowly absorbed back into the land and later a farmer will till this land and grow crops and the crops will feed the family and the family will grow up and old and no one will know that they used to be man. But this time the bones had been taken out, rearranged, put in a cedar box, the box was buried and his DNA cousins and children gathered around this box during a ritual to make sure it went underground. Flowers in bloom but cut off from the ground, therefore also dying, were placed around the box; one laid one upon another. And the DNA cousins and friends and children walked away whether it was raining or not and regretted what they never got to tell him. Like it would matter now if he had known just one more thing as an alive person.

Sometimes a man dies and his people gather around and eat chips and laugh about the things the dead man would do and say. His house was his crib and he never left it. His house was his African plain.

Sometimes someone dies and instead of putting the bone in your mouth the scientist finds semen on the panties.

When a human dies and that human was a Red Sox fan, sons, nephews, and grandchildren would deliver the newspaper on October 28, 2004 to the gravestone. This is a gesture of connection to the body that no longer has the spirit of the dead person inside of it. I rub my alive foot on the carcass.

This is the hind elephant foot tapping at the carcass. This is the lover rolling the body over to bring her back to life. This is the head lifted toward the sky trilling its trunk. This is looking at photographs of you and your grandparents trying to find a string between you. Here's a newspaper you can't read. This is what happens here on Earth and I don't need a bible. The sound I make dying is the sound I make when I was born. Shaking and pink, I last for ages.

When my uncle died

His sons put objects in his casket to be buried with him

Like photographs and baseball memorabilia.

This bothered me because the living needed these items.

He can't turn on the overhead light in his casket

Turn his neck and tap a photo of his wife

Before saying goodnight.

<u>O N E   W A Y   T O   W R I T E   A   S O N N E T</u>
<u>I S   T O   N U M B E R   T H E   L I N E S</u>

ONE WAY TO WRITE A SONNET IS TO NUMBER THE LINES

1. One way to give back to the previous generations is to allow
2. Elizabeth Barrett Browning to act as a wick, but yet hang liberally to her cake.
3. When learning how to drive the instructor said to me, "You're not
4. getting laid now, are you?" Well, he was right; I wasn't putting out.
5. "For my sake, stop holding the wheel too tight."
6. Though ungrateful at the time, I was indeed poverty stricken.
7. He saw how often I cried and held tight. He put the pillow under my head
8. and held the break pedal when necessary, and this is how to make
9. a three-point turn, and this is how to tell black from white and red from orange.
10. This is the method of falling asleep on a couch in a state of safety, and this is
11. falling asleep alone weeping in fear. Colors will make a better
12. blanket than the daily news. The colors will be steps to climb but better
13. than just falling asleep in front of the TV in cases of tiredness.
14. Proceed. Walk. Climb. Drive. This is called living.

ONE WAY TO WRITE A SONNET IS TO NUMBER THE LINES

1. Non-assholes deserve love. Assholes and
2. shitheads also deserve love. You deserve love.
3. Red fire burns the wax and adheres to the table.
4. It adheres to our expensive and old wood table.
5. Write this down in your dumb notebook: I love you.
6. Don't be embarrassed. This feeling is called being high.
7. We're high. In this state of ultimate control, I take my shirt off.
8. Too much art. Some of you love god. You are accepted by the masses.
9. I'm ready to cross the street and pat flesh. Then you will see
10. firsthand how love and nature seal each other forever.
11. America is a game I needn't play to understand.
12. Sidewalk shines on my face; the pavement makes crosses in my skin.
13. My knees buckle from love and what is going on in the x-snatch.
14. Where there was once a musical note is an orgasm dart.

ONE WAY TO WRITE A SONNET IS TO NUMBER THE LINES

1. Do I have the right to lay these gifts at your feet?

2. At the base of the same old tree,

3. my tears are saltier than yours because I'm aged.

4. You're watching my lips move but not paying attention.

5. Perhaps your eyes fall to my chest.

6. Why don't you smile as you educate like I do? Why are you

7. so afraid of happiness? The light falls through the trees

8. brightening your skin. You're alive! I gave you gifts,

9. but you gave me more gifts. Does that make me less generous?

10. You just regret sending that poisoned letter from Europe.

11. The one that made me bend over the toilet as I cried.

12. My love, I will keep filling this basket with love and presents.

13. Listen to what the fuck is coming out of my lips.

14. The minute hand marches on and so should you.

ONE WAY TO WRITE A SONNET
IS TO NUMBER THE LINES

1. Remember that time P sang

2. that Stones song—he pathologized this memory—

3. he'd have you think he was St. Francis with bird in hand.

4. I have known in my heart that I will die since I was young.

5. It's as difficult to live this way as it is for someone to be devout in all aspects,

6. Yay, once I blinked salt tears out of my eye,

7. I was looking back at those times—my sad, misspent youth.

8. And how this sick narcissist dominated my thunder.

9. The sun was not blocked by clouds.

10. So how did this sad person get my attention? He cried, whined,

11. pulled me like a cavewoman around with him. Total pig;

12. With confidence backing away, I asked:

13. "Who is this?"   P: "True Love?" Ha no.

14. A golden-voice answered, "Not love, but the folly of your youth."

ONE WAY TO WRITE A SONNET
IS TO NUMBER THE LINES

1. We thought only two people

2. heard what you said: the guy sitting beside

3. you and me. But a third person answered.

4. This guy who thought he was Jesus Christ.

5. As he spoke using his throat and his words, my face turned grey. I've lived in New York

6. too long—*he must be killed on the spot.* Could I wait three days?

7. His crucifixion alone would be a logistical nightmare.

8. I'm a relativist, so I just turned my glance to the subway floor. When "Jesus

9. Christ" said "Thank you" or "No" he tinged his words with a false ceremony.

10. As for us, we clutched our travel mugs and said nothing.

11. Christ on the L is just a Thursday morning;

12. Our hips and hands flattened into each others' crevices.

13. And all of heaven awaited his swearing corkscrew body.

14. I prayed to be hurled through the tunnel and even to the sky (if it were away from him).

ONE WAY TO WRITE A SONNET IS TO NUMBER THE LINES

1. We're from two worlds you fuckin gentleman.

2. A female and a male have different uses.

3. My crow and your wolf were taken off guard.

4. Your wolf went at my crow, but she saw him coming a mile away.

5. She dropped a feather to schedule Round Two. You think poetry

6. is something you get invited to formally, but it isn't.

7. I have collections of giant photos in which my tears are heavier than yours.

8. Your tears will be a good receptacle for my tears. Let's send my crow

9. and your wolf to acting classes. Piano lessons.

10. Why did you ask me for a light without looking at me?

11. Are you alone too?

12. Might we lean against the same tree?

13. I'll rub amber oil on your temples. Use water on me.

14. And we will stay there until some social media outlet finds us.

ONE WAY TO WRITE A SONNET IS TO NUMBER THE LINES

1. The world looks different like a face
2. not seen in years; now aged—fine-lines sagging
3. down these skins. Being with you is hung-over hearing a toddler run
4. back and forth in the rooms above. The ceiling beams and plaster
5. above my head troop death. I was in love and not paying attention
6. to anything, and now I'm left with debt. Drink baptismal water.
7. *Too weak to drink.* Telling you how cute your smile is
8. and how strong your arms are seems like Craigslist.
9. This water is blessed and sweet and wine.
10. Here are the names of birds I'd like to witness our nuptials:
11. lark, blue jay, hawk, and red herring. These are the instruments
12. that will make us cry: harp, flute, bass guitar, and drum.
13. The angel kneels watching us for three minutes. Then he gets up
14. and moves to the edge of the doorway so we can walk past.

ONE WAY TO WRITE A SONNET IS TO NUMBER THE LINES

1. Fuck off: I'm a poet. You ate my
2. emotional energy like cipher beetles
3. down my neck.
4. It's impossible to divide my mind
5. for a team. Or just very hard
6. to imagine a single life sighing its
7. way through without moving
8. Jupiter. Touch my hand. I'm crouching &
9. stealing lemons with my bio son.
10. An LOL, handled with care, will soon become a HA-HA-HA.
11. This wine tastes more ethereal than grapes.
12. Let's bring god before the courts. I'll mention your name
13. and soon enough cry *"Dos,"* pointing my middle fingers heavenward.
14. Without the sense of pain, he can make wines return to grapes.

SHADOW SELF

SHADOW SELF

In one version the steer stands in the doorway

trapping me.

In the other version there is no deer

but we have all fallen on the ground

strangled from the smoke pouring in through the windows.

I repeat – this is far worse than any pollution.

This is far worse than any pollution.

These are emotional times.

I am holding onto a string

when I am near you.

I grab a twelve-point buck.

I hold you around your chest.

Hold my neck out

for the catch.

BODY SCIENCE

My skin pushes water through itself

and Adam called this sweat and the water is called sweat.

My female parts void water from my bladder

and Adam called this urination and the water is called piss or pee.

My tear ducts excrete water

in conjunction with emotion

and this is called crying and the water is called tears.

Each carries different hormones, expels different substances.

I don't know what to call this feeling but I know you are mostly water too

and that you're gone from me.

M A Y F L Y

I.

My gutted, gutted face
mountains and mountaintops
inside. I'm inside you're outside.
Twins mirrored each other
You weren't seeing things.
You weren't seeing things.

Don't open that envelope.

II.

A regret is a sow.

III.

Buildings bulge.
When the building topples,
look inside at its cancer.
A large lime.
My gutted face
There was nothing inside me
except the occasional maggot,
the wet puppeteer of Oz.

Cut these cucumbers until there is no such thing as free will.

IV.

I live in a fifth floor walk-up.
The stairs are not steep.
I've been seduced on these stairs zero times.

I have cut myself on this large penis. It has bloomed and cut me.
letmein is my password for everything.

I've been betrayed
compromised.
The penis is my friend
I say *Hi you're my friend you know you're my friend.*
It says *We're at war god damn it. Close the door.*

She storms offstage enraged but still gets the part.

My gutted face holds flora within its fauna.
Pupa within a large corpse-flower
smells like the most beautiful
perfume you could ever possibly imagine:
I'm dead! I smell great! Hold me! Hold me, Sow, hold me!
We're in love! We're in love! You love everything about me!

BARREN WILDERNESS

see the world for what it is

maybe the subtlety   of the dry branches reaching to the hawks

with bony hands

life is a marathon/a sprint

snow looks designed

by filmmakers

to extend the mood

don't put a crow there

without awareness

it will block the foreground

of any given food trough

wolves gather and kill

with their dream-catchers

and may hear

the stomping of man

from miles away

but this will not prevent

the shadows from falling

onto their own faces

i'm talking about

the characters on tarot cards

the long swift hair in the hand

of a light blue man

we travel to heaven/hell in a biplane designed for *us*

The bearded man sometimes shaves his beard

so arms might swell and lock around his neck

long ago man would drink until he remembered   nothing of the previous evening

to succeed in each marathon

and as the wolves chill around

the buffalo

it's like he never even had a chance

i think of how they drain

they wander around

shuffling, sprinting

the buffalo runs the marathon of his life

and maybe

if he drank

a twelve pack

last night

he'd be dumbtired enough

dumbtired enough to sprint

like his captors

i am in a marathon

i see the little bunny with the black eyes

i am seen by the white wolf with the same

the wolf with its fur loosened up

i can see my wolf

i can see how i might die upright   i bend my head back

into camel posture

i must rough my back through these young nettles

to rid my fur/enjoy the arrival of the young

the arctic wolf in summer is an old man

who does not see the piece of food

stuck to his chin

and though brutal in his honesty

has not a proper vessel to fill his offal

this time the hills are dried lava

overlaid with brown grass

the buffalo communication systems

mourn death

but don't know how

to keep life   as unique as webs

when a wolf is at hunt

she forms a straight line

buff protects kin

in a phalanx an opening forms within the chattel

spelling the word R E G R E T on the marquis

we ride off toward the trees

and grab the baby down

to feed the whole tribe high

we pull him to the ground

and are fed all day

the wolves' eyes are yellow

with desire

and I wonder if there is a place

where never must i want

and never must i play

i wonder if there will be a day   when i might remain

take the yellow from my eyes

let me just look back

i look online

and see so much decay

desire what i may

shopping trip/man/writer/buffalo

a young arctic wolf drowns the buff

with her large hard jaw   dialoguing with his neck

other wolves rub their backs

on the charred grass

it takes many generations for man to recover from

forest fire

but for now   it's an exfoliation brush

sometimes men put wolf hides onto their backs

to impersonate wolves

and spook the buff   round the other side

and kill

when you kill a buffalo/an adult without cancer

it's difficult to imagine

how scared the animal must be

last scared glare/long borrowed teeth/head pulled away

and only a psychopath would want to do this stuff

so i'm wondering whether a wolf is a psychopath

and i remember watching a documentary about a serial killer

and think better of the wolf

and after that

we arch our backs

and expect to be gotten off by our partners

because our partners love us

and we love us

you love us

and i remain

a puppy/puppet in play

without the internet

but my salt lick

has restorative qualities

like your lick

and if we have a body of water near us

sex can be fun

an urge

pedestal that creaks/a braid too tickly/a man who looks like a man

but acts like the woman/a man who does what he came for

and will be back

and when he comes back

he'll bring bread

just don't put him in a cage

a cage makes a wolf/man go nuts

and take my key

and turn the master lock

and let the wolf out

because he has learned his lesson

like i learned my lesson

many years ago

when will did not change things

because I could not change things

i don't have access to your rectangle

but i can turn and back away from those

who are sad and without hope

i can smile

i might touch

but eventually i might have to back away

and bring by some ice cream once so things aren't too awkward

but then back away

slowly

and without haste

i want the wolves to all be happy

and when I hold the lightning rod in the air

with my bare hand

i hope that he says *please take care*

ranchers have been lost and the wolves were blamed

so honey pull your arm down from the sky

and be a pisces

and lay down

and lay you down

no be an air sign

and he comforts

when the monsoon comes

a black buck jumps like a flea on a hound

pups engage in light oral play

and the adults react to this surprise by stealing livestock

everyone is taken care of

but no one is happy

we are filled with the regret

of being alone together

but hopefully some fresh sheep come to town

who will encourage new conversation

and protection of the other wilderness—the one in here—heart

And when the car is out of gas

one of us will walk

one will shake and heave in ecstatic throes

i can only have six pigs suckling on me at once

five really if I were honest with myself

to be an authority/a ham

are processes that happen

against the better wishes of the authority herself

a click in a brain

a brain changes into a brian

and brian will turn off the lights at the end of the night

fold a blanket until it folds no more

speak into the microphone to the authority

the author talks back

in the cities the wolves must be cautious

but that's ok because the wolves observe

and learn and change

they will back out and black out

the olive gas and the perfect credit

help achieve that desired eventuality

a butt on a wolf is not a butt

to be grabbed and smacked

with gentle cuddle and cup

don't bruise the very thing

that got you here

a car is out of place

in the wolf's ken

a dumb double-spaced dog

is not heard

and can't keep up with a wolf

even if he sees their similarities

a mountain is witness to a similar buttfuck

and in order to survive

one must

not let the wolves into the buildings of man

lest

a consort with a car and a weapon

should take her down for good

she can take care of herself

she can stray

and should there be strangers

who desire my daughter's fur

i will make chum of them

a sturdy dirty kind of chum

that makes rent

and alienates friends

THIS IS AN EXAMPLE
OF MY FUNCTIONALITY

My blood flows from heart to legs to toes back to heart. My foreshortening is fucked. Always too soon. I'm in the shadow… I mean I'm in the shower. When my neck has been washed, I wash my shoulders. Oh my god I'm so alone. I will never find a way to tell you how pale I am. I am too pale. Rubbing my arm, rubbing my arm. Other body parts. When I close my eyes, I see my blood inside my eyelids and the air and the room. This feels semi-public. I am in a tank. The tank is five foot ten. It covers me like a glove, a glove with a large butt. Shut the fuck up with your purple eyeshadow.

When the sun sets, we will shower again. I don't know what to do without this pool of grain surrounding me. A beach, the Australian crawl, figuring out the math for piss in chlorine and still being clean. When I was a toddler my sister Molly and I took a bath together. We splashed. I pooped. She was alarmed in a way I did not recognize from the times I had peed in the tub. I mean—it was just me.

PORTICO

You drew me onto a portico and said *This is for you*. It was a beautiful necklace—rock hanging below cardinal numbers zero through nine. I held it and *Thank you*. You sat on a bench. Walls closed around us like in a car. It felt better than kissing some people but worse than kissing others. *You can do whatever you want*, you said. This was an explicit reference to your penis. I held it and said *This is bigger than you've led me to believe it would be. You can do whatever you want with it*, you said. I stroked it, your eyes appealed. First, I picked off a fine piece of crust.

PURIFICATION TEST

One girl was simply
shot in the chest, then in the hands, then between her eyes
with bullets so light and quick the sounds she made
were the sounds women's mouths make when pounded too hard
during love-making.

Some of us, who were asked to change into radiation suits in the vestibule,
were later injected with a serum that paralyzed our bodies.
My crazy ex-boyfriend told me about this. "It happens right before the anal probe."
"That's when they extract the information they need
from your brain." My body limp. I wondered if my eyes looked
as frightened as I was.
I stuck to the facts. I had no opinions.
I literally have no opinions—just many many
experiences. Yes, I freed the lion from the zoo.
He was tired of his confines. I freed that prisoner from jail. He was innocent
and was not supposed to die. I ran over the rich in
W_____. They were voting wrong. I robbed that bank and that bank and that bank.
Some of us, who were wearing
the radiation suits, paralyzed, answering questions were told to open our eyes.
Open your eyes. *I can't see*. But now I can see it. I have no opinions.
But I agree: salt and pepper *are* exotic spices.

CANNIBAL WEDDING

When two cannibals start dating, they're just like us. First awkward date includes coffee or alcohol. Maybe some furious necking in a cab or in the hallway near the restroom. When she got home, she looked in the mirror and she looked the same as yesterday. But in her own eyes she saw something different. She saw who he saw. Aristophanes' creation myth was never considered, but its blueprint was etched inside her skull. When two cannibals continue seeing each other seriously, it's no different from when you started dating your lover. The bathroom door is kept closed during use even though the conversations were so damned interesting and hard to pull away from. Sheets are washed at such rapid pace from wear, at least one cannibal cancels a long-held gym membership. One cannibal says, *You make me a better person*. This makes the other cannibal cry. Their mouths meld together wet with tears. The feast was quite fine. To quote August Wilson, the cannibals *try to blast a hole into forever*. They stay in all weekend continuing a decently organized search-and-destroy mission that always ends in a self-absorbed celebration. But when one cannibal finds out that the other cannibal was still fucking his ex for the first month they were seeing each other, the cannibals stop seeing each other. Thankfully, the erring cannibal certainly knows enough about how Hollywood defines romance to show up unannounced with flowers and cries his heart out until their mouths pressed together sticky with tears, and they decide (with their breasts, penises, vaginas and assholes, mouths and eyes) to face infinity together. At the cannibal wedding those invited looked upon them. Those who had loved and lost cried. And those who had never loved but wanted to love cried. And she, who had looked inside herself and knew that it's just fucking wrong to expect another person to fill one's vessel, cried too because she was the loneliest. She was the one person whose heart needed to be eaten the most.

MY DEAD

I'm a poet but doesn't that just mean
I'm giving up some necessities
to make room for more difficult things?
A really dark place opened up.
Busy/occupied,
the voice got quieter for a few minutes.
Now it's back– a rare 45 loud as hell
all snap and grain–
but it's no book of answers.
It has no light.
It has no body rested against it.
For a few minutes before I sank
into the chair in a really dark place
I thought there must be people like me
and there are. A couple
of Elizabeth Bishop's lovers killed themselves
and people don't talk enough about that.
That's what Amanda said. *People need to talk more about that.*
The beautiful leaves on the ground are just that – beautiful.
The color, yes, transports us. But little else.
On the ground, it does nothing;
it will just get uglier and uglier
and that's what could happen to you.
One time I took a sad walk while I was in a sad relationship and I thought
some really sad things and I'm glad that was all it was.

It's important to feel like shit sometimes.

If you don't, you may be totally wrong and dead and I don't know what would happen the

ROBERT FROST

Unable to eat all of his own children,
Robert Frost
would tuck us in again after we'd gone to bed.
He'd say
Here is warm milk.
Consider how even this mug will eventually disintegrate
like my mother who used to bathe her
fake teeth in it before she died.
He even took my ability to mourn for
my grandmother.

Once I saw him with a balled-up hanky in his mouth
sucking his own spit as he wrote, moaning into the cloth.
I grabbed a log
to put it over the dying embers in the fireplace.
He grabbed it out
of my hands and said it wasn't cold enough.

SUNT PUERI PUERI, PUERI PUERILIA TRACTANT

I try to keep people from knowing
a bucked-up deer came in my window.

I live on the fifth floor
where things that are sad are laughed at and vice versa.

That didn't mean what I meant it to.
I might still be high from two nights ago.

I listen to the Kinks. Then I come up with words
that mean hunger and loneliness, a deer used for physical purposes.

It's easier to take that hardhat and put it under my shirt
grab your hand and make you feel it baby.

THE SHAPE OF SPAIN'S FLAG

After the volcano, all the victims subsisted on what came out of the volcano. We call them Ash-eaters. I take an Ash-eater and he climbs the stairs into my bedroom. Then the next night, he sleeps on the couch. Then there are more and more. They can't all be properly fed and satisfied. They got out of control. During insomnia, I think of Marc Summers from Double Dare. He's OCD and washes his hands like a thousand times a day. The river. I wonder if he washed his hands in the river. But he would be too stressed about bacteria. When there was a gunshot, the deer stopped farting and munching grass, looked back then sprang away away, like Nazis, away. The Ash-eaters tell me the devastation is real. They tell me the ash in my kitchen is real. One has brown oil smudged in the shape of Spain's flag. I tell that one he's an idiot. He was in my bed looking at me like a zombie who doesn't know he's a zombie yet. I ran downstairs and emailed him to get out.

THEY STILL MAKE MOHAMMED ALI POSE WITH CLENCHED FISTS

What happened once still happens even though the players are aged, and we no longer want to see them do this, the position creaky in the key of atrophy.

It is now almost time for your nap, Mohammed.

I'm on the edge, I know.

He should get to sit in his recliner.
He would be easily photographed like that,
chillin with his legs up,
and you'd think Oh wow. He must watch some pretty good TV.

PAIN MINUS LOVE EQUALS PAIN

I made some mistakes in my life.
I solved one by one.
Puzzles me to watch a white man
holding a young girl. An animal
riding a squirrel. I'm walking along the path
crying for still. I eat the forest with my eyes.
You're empty for breakfast.
You're empty for lunch.
You eat me for dinner.
I eat the lush forest trees with my eyes
and crouch down and bite mossy growth
with my mouth
spitting up my previous dinner.

EASILY AS YOUR HEART

Oh this doom so gentle

as to fit you in my hand

so cheap, so far away.

Must it stray so easily

as your heart from she

you had affixed to

with such adhesive apathy.

She smiles beside you

does not know

the clamping

thighs, no none must know.

And in the middle of the night

head to the bathroom *just to pee*

Your hand arises (familiar now)

tightens to milk a cow

close your eyes

and tug it off

every thirty seconds

peeking soft at self

into the mirror thus—no no

not so rough—

to see how you would look with me

were I your hand

and also

your other hand.

WHAT NOURISHES ME DESTROYS ME

I.

You said calling me was visiting my grave.

I hereby demand a fence around my grave.

When we drive our scooters along the Great Wall of China

I hear a special ring in my ears, a storm, not unlike reincarnation.

Next spring it will feel the same

when we again rub our scooters down the Great Wall of China.

Beguile me all you like. I'm a genius; the future steps of my feet

make bugle sounds. When I touch you it's devil's food cake in church.

II

Open the window and yell no. You're still afraid.

I speak to you from beyond the grave. But that doesn't mean

nothing for nothing. I'm taking the surface roads. You're

in a really sad place curled up in a casket. I have a famous laugh you hear

miles away. Yes, we die alone but that's no reason

to cancel the party.

There's a stranger crashing on my couch. I keep pouring

tea down his shirt to wake him up. What a mess.

I'm not dancing too hard over where your head would be.

THE OLD SHALL INHERIT
THE YOUNG

AFTER BAUDELAIRE

The woods made me crap myself.
You hear that, woods?
The silence, prolonged, hurts me
the way yearning for a giant building
ruined that rich sheik in Dubai.
A forest stifles itself
when no one is there.
M. Night Shyamalan
hurts his audiences;
hunts me the way the Vatican hunts for Vatican cash.
I am sentenced to hell.

The ocean made me crap myself.
I'm crying like a baby just
crying salt water.
If I were crying for you I'd
cry mini versions of you.
This is an Irish Funeral in the Gulf,
which means there's a party
in the dead person's home.
Shotgun a beer next to a slicked gull
next to Ned the tuna's fetid fin.

Night is ugly as all the other shit
I just mentioned.
I am holding a mirror up so you can see how
ridiculous you look in that outfit:
I can't see any stars so how do I even know it's night?

MY DEAD

The car exploded for some political reason

I saw a monkey falling asleep in the water

a monk meditating and praying

a girl doing laundry

a miniature hat or maybe the Torah on the head of a man

a baby with a cone head looking for his mother

rugging his head against an empty palm

I saw you look right hiding, hiding

I saw bugs in the bed that were just asterisks

An old man staring at the fire

counting rosary beads

but not praying

and the cancer patient is bald

yet still hopeful

We put our hands together

and thought of religion

We make billboards with slanty eyes or white yeses

Between two rocks comes the water

Moses can't save you now

Never saved you

I saw the big girl rock

and climbed it

I will bring you the lettuce

my dead

but I will carry it on my head my dead

We've been praying like this for many generations

Architecture is an act of prayer

Let's gather around this statue we made

and create a beautiful energy

I'll put a flower behind my ear, my dead

Let's follow the man without hair

He's happier than the others

but has no teeth

A volcano was born

with drums inside

The earth has first-degree burns

The smoke is coming

for me

The line in the earth starts smoking upward

the lesson has been taught when it retreats

Look through it when it parts

and see the grand creations

the passage of time

like you're bigger than yourself

Look through at the red rocks

and the sun

The Earth made tiki torches first

when it made an octopus

and a lizard with the bodies of old men

laying about in the dusk

flapping skin

and dry heat

My body is red too

but I don't look ancient

My spikes absorbed back inside my spine

I live inside my apartment

Eventually man came over to this rock

and drew pictures of himself

A little boy with his hair shaved down close like a monk's

And why do we dance?

Your weird ears

absent necklace

little goose-stepping babies

backward breast brown nipple painted tattoo ink

Now that you've prepared, we can speak of the baggy

red diapers

all men wear

Thank god we're not in the factories any more

Being homeless

is all in your head, man

Homes are man-made

Let's get out of our heads, man

You got your towel, you got your watch, what more do you need?

The rhetoric of jammies with footsies

The little midget pan-faced kids

The boy whose face is buried in grammy's lace curtain

trades money for sex and sex for money

The old Japanese art of white face

The newer, hipper Japanese art of underpants riding up during dinner

Giant planes

all lined up in the largest airbase you can imagine

Here is the border

This is where they don't listen to world music

Holler back to me when the fire goes out   I'm so jammed up

like a cactus that's had the shit kicked out of it

by a match

Hang the lead pipe from your neck because *This Means War!*

is our heavy ass command rule

Had to put some dirt into the pizza oven

which we'd conveniently forgotten about

to make it smell like we're eating somewhere else

I used to be one of those cowboys who wore the specialty glasses

that allowed purview of canaries in tubes

and canaries in mines

This was where the enemy took your photo

Before they burned you to a crisp

This is what it sounds like to be treated like a pit

This is what it means to meditate

This is how healthy I am

and this is a monk ringing a bell

He hits the bell in a special circle

This prayer is a jump

My teeth are white

I keep it that way

This week I have been struck by an intense and agonizing fear of death. I don't know what it means but *I can not die*, at least not any time soon. Something is on the line. It's incredibly terrifying to me and I can think of nothing else. There is something on the line for all of us, naturally. However, at this juncture a lot is on the line and I speak of the personal, intellectual, historical, spiritual, emotional, and universal all at once. It is by pure chance and also by no chance at all that my fear of death has arrived at this time.

Having a fear of death has, I suppose, been with us this whole time but now I feel it. The fear is no longer implicit, a parasite has come to form. It is terrifying, and I don't know what to do as a human, as a woman, writer, or as any part of my plurality. Perhaps the identities I have placeholders for are not enough to contain the idea of *to belong*. The mind desires to add another mother, wife, scientist, hermit. Fear of death is why women wear make up, why men wear toupees, why the young dance, and why we, the fertile, pitch woo and do things with bodies to other bodies that involve sweat and shame and a degree of mental castration. This is something in all of us: to preserve something leaving, but dependent upon time and space. The arrival of the fear is the arrival of one adulthood. However, some people never become adults.

This morning I saw a blossomed bulb of flowers concurrently dying and blossoming. It was, I believed, a hydrangea. It was one of those beautiful blues that we associate with fresh baby boys and wide summer skies. And there it was. Each petal both in bloom & new, but also dried out and browned from a recent heat wave in Brooklyn. I wish there were a word in the English language that meant "fuck me/bye-bye," for that word would capture what I experienced in those flowers.

I saw a woman hit by a cab in the street in the dead of night some seven months ago, and seeing her shake—seeing the LIFE shake out of her is something that I can't pretend not to know. It was a sudden dance in the air which changed its stage onto the ground, and as her husband called out *Anna I love you don't go* just like one might say to one's partner as he or she leaves for work in the morning: quiet and urgent and even erotic, it implied a station, a place where we might stay, and yet also a place where we might travel to. It occurred slow and fast like when my friend Carter fell back in a plastic chair the other night on my roof deck. We laughed as Carter wound his arms as he fell like he was trying to fly. But as we laughed, he fell, and as he fell, we also wanted to save him from falling, and as we wanted to save him, we also feared for his safety due to the proximity to the roof's ledge. And through our fear and the lot of it, he still continued to attempt to tell a short aside that added immeasurably to a conversation we'd been having about my sex life. Many things at once may slow down time and add layers of meaning to our interactions. Perspective is our meek station. *Anna I love you don't go.*

The other night at a bar I decided that my fear of death would be an appropriate conversation starter, and boy, was I right. Sometimes a friend will allow him/herself to speak. Sometimes this friend won't speak on his fear of death. Sometimes it is because it doesn't interest this person. Sometimes I speak like a self-inflated bore. Sometimes I am in jocular good spirits. In the course of dialogue with a third or fourth friend, I recognized the possibility that my fear of death was, specifically, related to my own understanding of certain unfulfilled personal accomplishments—the selfish antagonist: my own ego. This totally crushed me, as you might imagine. This journey so fresh and devastating and visceral and physical: might it really just be a clown mirror highlighting certain parts of my mind? Was it never about imagining my brain in a jar with an "Out of Service" sign hung from it? Was it never about being too scared to watch horror movies alone for fear of being killed by an unknown "monster"? Was it a taxonomy of self? I steeled myself, looked again at my silent traveler, and resolved that part of the fear of death is its giant scope, its imperative and interpretive nature, its changeability. It morphs over time, but it should not be dripped out steadily like an IV, but measured delicately with a glass tincture, for the human mind is limited in its multitudes and one should not be expected to live daily facing the very thing it is working so hard to avoid doing—and yet anyone who's ever crossed a street knows that this is, in fact, natural to the animal mind.

On a recent evening I attended a barbeque with family members. Most of those in attendance were adults. However, the children commanded the widest attention bandwidth. The hostess, who wore a yellow Hawaiian lei, taught her granddaughter how to hula hoop. If the children don't get our attention they might perish. But if I give a child all of my attention, I will certainly perish. Where is the space here for adults to play with their own thoughts, where is reason, where may I communicate with an adult about adult things? Just yesterday I wrote to a friend: *We must attempt to find a meaning--if not in poetry then somewhere else in our lives*. At the time I meant to bring him cheer in his own work. But now it brings me my own comfort—teaching a toddler how to hula hoop is meaningful. This is the family recipe for pie dough. Here is how to wash your face. This is what biting into a Cheerio with no teeth feels like. Here is how to remove wallpaper from a good wall. Here is how to remove wallpaper from walls with soft plaster. Shrink and shrink and shrink. It is terrifying for me to think of those who feel they have nothing of value to share. In the presence of the younger generation I consider with pride the ideas I would like to share.

During a walk outside on Wednesday I read the very poem you are reading as I walked toward a class I'd promised to teach. My chin was tucked toward my chest. My sunglasses turned crisp whites into dung browns. About to step my foot onto a deserted street, a black BMW hurled past me *out of nowhere*. It certainly did not come from "nowhere." It came from somewhere. My perspective is a meek station. I looked up from these pages, folding them into my bag, and walked onward paying slightly more attention to my physical surroundings. Almost dead from considering my own art which had birthed from a consideration of my own death. *Anna I love you don't go.*

I noticed men at work creating those drilling sounds. I noticed cicadas don't quiet down in accordance with my desires. An ego does not spill back into its vessel at the same rate at which a head of hair is stripped of its pigment.

I asked my mother the name of the flower and she said *hydrangea*.

A C K N O W L E D G E M E N T S

Thank you to the following journals in which some of the poems have appeared, sometimes in altered form: *Pax Americana*, *Forklift, Ohio*, *Sink Review*, *On the Escape*, *Smalldoggies Magazine*, *LIT*, *BlazeVOX*, *The Nepotist*, *Gigantic*, *Bling That Sings*, *Everyday Genius*, *Catch Up*, *Lyre Lyre*, *Scapegoat Review*, and *Octopus Magazine*.

Elephants in Mourning was originally published as a chapbook by [sic] Press.

Two poems from "One Way to Write a Sonnet Is to Number the Lines" first appeared in a pamphlet published by Greying Ghost Press.

The poems entitled "One Way to Write a Sonnet Is to Number the Lines" owe much to Elizabeth Barrett Browning's *Sonnets from the Portuguese*.

"Barren Wilderness" is for Paige Taggart.

Thank you to my family.

Thank you Jackie Clark, Ryan Doyle May, B.C. Edwards, Ted Dodson, Ben Fama, Sasha Fletcher, Alina Gregorian, Matt Hart, Dan Hoy, Lauren Hunter, Jennifer L. Knox, Christine Kanownik, David Lehman, Dan Magers, Monica McClure, Ben Mirov, Alex Smith, Sampson Starkweather, Amanda Smeltz, Paige Taggart, Maggie Wells, and Angela Veronica Wong for your support, inspiration, help with poems in this manuscript and for your friendship.

Thank you Mathias Svalina, Alisa Heinzman, Zachary Schomburg, Drew Scott Swenhaugen, and everyone at Octopus Books for your brilliant insights, support, humor, and everything in the editing, creation, and design of this book.

OCTOPUS

is a small press poetry publishing organization comprised of four departments: OCTOPUS BOOKS, a full-length poetry press; OCTOPUS MAGAZINE, an online poetry journal; POOR CLAUDIA, the chapbook imprint; and BAD BLOOD, an occasional reading series based in Portland, Oregon. These four departments merged in August 2012 in order to focus on the unending possibilities of how poetry can be encountered. Each department is autonomous, but the organization in its entirety is collaborative and democratic. Each department has different submission and publishing policies that can be read on each corresponding website:

OCTOPUSBOOKS.NET

OCTOPUSMAGAZINE.COM

POORCLAUDIA.ORG

BADBLOODPOETRY.ORG